Wales Coast Path
Coastal **Pub Walks:** North Wales

AF066852

Text: Carl Rogers

Series editor: Tony Bowerman

Photographs: Carl Rogers, Tony Bowerman, Alamy, Adobe Stock, Dreamstime, Shutterstock

Design: Carl Rogers and Laura Hodgkinson

© Northern Eye Books Limited 2021

Carl Rogers has asserted his rights under the Copyright, Designs and Patents Act, 1988 to be identified as the author of this work. All rights reserved.

This book contains mapping data licensed from the Ordnance Survey with the permission of the Controller of Her Majesty's Stationery Office. © Crown copyright 2021 All rights reserved. License number 100047867

Northern Eye Books
ISBN 978-1-908632-82-1

A CIP catalogue record for this book is available from the British Library.

Printed in the UK

Cover: *Tŷ Coch, Porth Dinllaen, Llŷn (Walk 6)*

Important Advice: The routes described in this book are undertaken at the reader's own risk. Walkers should take into account their level of fitness, wear suitable footwear and clothing, and carry food and water. It is also advisable to take the relevant OS map with you in case you get lost and leave the area covered by our maps.

Whilst every care has been taken to ensure the accuracy of the route directions, the publishers cannot accept responsibility for errors or omissions, or for changes in the details given. Nor can the publisher and copyright owners accept responsibility for any consequences arising from the use of this book.

If you find any inaccuracies in either the text or maps, please write or email us at the address below. Thank you.

First published in 2021 by:

Northern Eye Books Limited
Northern Eye Books, Tattenhall, Cheshire CH3 9P?

tony@northerneyebooks.co.uk

www.northerneyebooks.co.uk

 @northerneyebooks
@wales_coast_path
@carlrogers1960

 @northerneyeboo
@WalesCoastUK

For sales enquiries, please call 01928 723 744

www.walescoastpath.co.uk

MIX
Paper from responsible sources
FSC® C016379

Contents

The Wales Coast Path 4

Top 10 Walks: North Wales' best coastal pubs 6

1 | **The Snowdon**, *Llandudno* 8

2 | **Erskine Arms**, *Conwy* 14

3 | **Ship Inn**, *Red Wharf Bay* 20

4 | **White Eagle**, *Rhoscolyn* 24

5 | **Oystercatcher**, *Rhosneigr* 30

6 | **Tŷ Côch Inn**, *Porth Dinllaen* 36

7 | **Tŷ Newydd**, *Aberdaron* 42

8 | **Sun Inn**, *Llanengan* 48

9 | **Glyn y Weddw Arms**, *Llanbedrog* 54

10 | **Yr Awstralia**, *Porthmadog* 58

Useful Information 64

The Wales Coast Path

WALES IS THE ONLY COUNTRY IN THE WORLD with a path around its entire coast. The long-distance Wales Coast Path offers 870 miles/1400 kilometres of unbroken coastal walking, from the outskirts of the ancient walled city of Chester in the north to the Georgian market town of Chepstow in the south.

There's something new around every corner. Visually stunning and rich in both history and wildlife, the path promises ever-changing views, wildflowers and seabirds, as well as castles, coves and coastal pubs.

In fact, the Wales Coast Path runs through 1 Marine Nature Reserve, 2 National Parks, 3 Areas of Outstanding Natural Beauty, 11 National Nature Reserves, 14 Heritage Coasts, and 23 Historic Landscapes.

And, to cap it all, the **Wales Coast Path** links up with the long-distance Offa's Dyke Path at either end: creating a complete, 1,030 mile circuit of the whole of Wales.

Beer on the beach at Porth Dinllaen

North Wales' coastal pubs

What could be better than a bracing coastal walk followed by a pint and maybe a meal in an authentic Welsh pub by the sea? All the pubs in the following pages are situated either right on the coast (there are even two right on the shore) or a short distance inland and almost every one is open all day.

The walks, too, are carefully chosen and take in circuits that embrace some of the very best bits of the world-beating Wales Coast Path — including medieval castles, steam trains, deserted beaches, a holy island and a fantasy village.

Along the way, you'll discover fine Welsh beers and ales, locally caught seafood, and characterful Welsh pubs and inns. These are days by the sea that will live on in your memory for years to come.

Welsh: "Ti'n mynd i'r dafarn?"
English: "Are you going to the pub?"

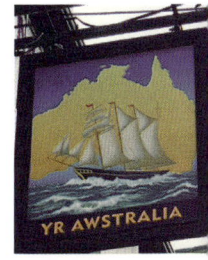

TOP 10 Walks: North Wales' best coastal Pub Walks

EACH OF THE SELECTED CIRCULAR WALKS incorporates a stretch of the Wales Coast Path, with most starting and finishing close to a superb coastal pub. Combined they cover the very best stretches of North Wales' coastline, one of great natural beauty and variety. Needless to say, tourist honeypots like Llandudno and Porthmadog can get busy, but once away from the towns you can always escape the crowds on the Wales Coast Path. With the pubs open all year and the walking good in all seasons, the North Wales' coast is a true year-round destination.

Snowdon Llandudno — page 8

Erskine Arms Conwy — page 14

Ship Inn Red Wharf Bay — page 20

White Eagle Rhoscolyn — page 24

Oystercatcher Rhosneigr — page 30

Tŷ Coch Porth Dinllaen — page 36

Tŷ Newydd Aberdaron — page 42

Sun Inn Llanengan — page 48

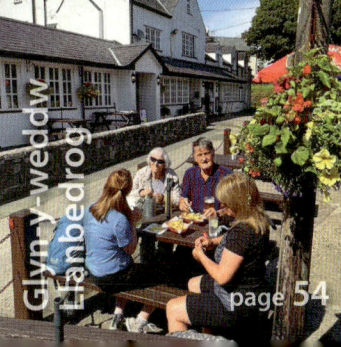

Glyn-y-weddw Llanbedrog — page 54

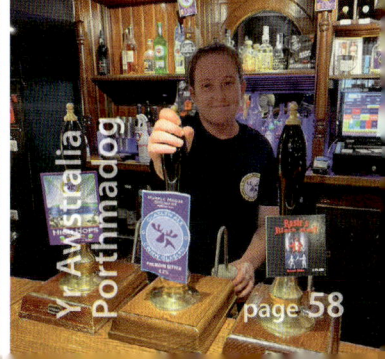

Yr Awstralia Porthmadog — page 58

The Snowdon

North Wales Coast

The Snowdon
Llandudno

walk 1

What to expect: *Good paths through town and over hilly ground with grand views*

Distance/time: 8 kilometres/ 5 miles. Allow 3 hours
Start: Parking is available at various points around the town, notably along West Parade. Begin the walk beside the pub in Tudno Street at the northern end of the town.
Grid ref: SY 779 826
Ordnance Survey map: OS Explorer OL17 Snowdon/Yr Wyddfa - *Conwy Valley/Dyffryn Conwy*
The Pub: The Snowdon, 11 Tudno Street, Llandudno LL30 2HB | 01492 872 166 | www.thesnowdon.co.uk

Walk outline: From the northern end of Llandudno, good urban paths take you up through the gardens of Happy Valley and onto the contrasting open hilltop of the Great Orme, with its wide panoramas along the coast and inland to the hills of Snowdonia. Good paths through farmland and open limestone grassland lead around the Orme high above the sea, with a steep descent back into Llandudno.

One of the oldest pubs in Llandudno, The Snowdon sits at the end of a Victorian terrace slightly above the town. The building dates from the early 1800s when it served the Great Orme's thirsty mining community. Today, this cosy and atmospheric pub serves a great range of cask ales and wines, and quality lunchtime food.

The Snowdon

▶ The Snowdon at a glance

Open: Daily 11.30pm-11pm
Brewery/company: Stange & Co, Llandudno
Ales and wine: Good selection of quality cask ales; wide choice of wines
Food: Monday - Tuesday 12 noon - 3pm. Wednesday - Sunday 12 noon - 6pm. Good menu of classic pub dishes. Nibbles, light bites, mains, puddings and vegetarian. Sorry, no reservations
Children & dogs: Both very welcome. Children's menu and highchairs available
Outside: Heated sun terrace at the front of the pub

The Walk

1. Facing the pub, go left along the road and turn right at the T-junction. Immediately after the **Empire Hotel**, turn left along **Tŷ Gwyn Road**. On the bend bear right along **Hill Terrace** and at the end of the road go up steps on the right. Follow the path past the **cable car station** and down steps to reach a little roundabout by the café.

Cross over and turn left up the footpath with the road on your left. At the top of the green, turn right and follow the path to the right-hand side of the **gardens**.

Don't go through the gate here, instead, go left on the footpath which follows the right-hand edge of the gardens. There are occasional waymark posts indicating the way to 'The Summit'.

At the very top of the gardens go through a gate to the right of a stone shelter.

Follow the footpath up beside the **ski slope** on the left. Near the top of the rise there are **steps beside a wall** on the left. At the top of the steps turn right and walk over the grass for a few metres to a fine viewpoint over Llandudno Bay.

This is one of the finest viewpoints in the area giving a grand panorama over much of the town, and east towards the Little

© Crown copyright and/or database right. All rights reserved. Licence number 100047867

A section of limestone pavement on the Great Orme

Orme. Beyond lie the resorts of Colwyn Bay and Rhyl with the Clwydian Range on the skyline. In very clear conditions the tip of Wirral and the Lancashire coast can occasionally be seen.

To the south beyond Llandudno, are Conwy Mountain and the headlands of Penmaenbach and Penmaenmawr out to the west. Beyond these foothills, the higher tops of the Carneddau rise to Carnedd Llywelyn, Wales' second highest summit.

Rejoin the path at the top of the steps beside the wall. At the end of the wall keep ahead on the signed path to 'St Tudno's Church'. This curves over the rounded hillside and soon the **summit complex** comes into view ahead. There is more than one footpath here but keep ahead, soon with a **walled field** on the right. Just before a **farmhouse** turn right through a large kissing gate and follow a fenced path past the farm and then ahead on a path between fields. The path eventually reaches the little **church of St Tudno**, situated on a green terrace overlooking the sea.

2. Turn left up the lane. At the top of the rise and at the far end of a lay-by, turn right and follow a **track** as it contours the hillside.

The wide panorama from the Great Orme west towards Snowdonia and Anglesey

On either side of this track are traces of medieval field systems along with the outlines of two groups of long huts higher up the slope. Of particular note are the prehistoric mines which have proved to be one of the most important examples of Bronze Age mining in the country.

Follow the track with a **high stone wall** on your left for 1.5 kilometres/1 mile.

Eventually, at the top of a rise on the west side of the Orme, there is a **ruined stone cairn** on the right with a fine view out over Conwy Bay.

3. The path continues beside the wall and in 300 metres or so, look for a path which bears right descending a little before contouring the steep hillside. There is more than one path here but don't be tempted to to descend to lower paths visible below.

After passing high above **large houses** and **gardens** on the very edge of the sea below, the path curves leftwards onto a grassy shoulder with a bird's eye view over Llandudno. A little further on the path passes the **corner of a field** on the left. Stay beside the wall ignoring minor paths on the right. At **houses** on the left where there is a **bench** overlooking the town, the waymarked path 'To Town' turns right and zigzags steeply down the hillside.

4. At the bottom of the slope the path joins a tarmac footpath with a **stone shelter** to the right. Turn left along this path which eventually passes through a small park ('Haulfre Gardens') to join **Cwalch Road**. At the end of the road turn right down a narrow side road to reach the town. Cross the road and go ahead along **Llewelyn Avenue**. At **Tudno Street** turn left reach The Snowdon. ♦

Feral goats

A herd of around 200 white Kashmir goats have long been an integral part of Llandudno's Great Orme. Originally the property of Lord Mostyn — who was given a pair by Queen Victoria — the goats have been feral for more than a century. Their constant browsing on even the steepest slopes helps maintain the limestone headland's unique mixture of plants and insects — including rockrose, wild cotoneaster bushes and rare silver-studded blue butterflies. During lockdown in 2020, they became famous for wandering Llandudno's empty streets.

The Erskine Arms in the centre of Conwy

North Wales Coast

The Erskine Arms
Conwy

walk 2

What to expect:
Good hill and coast paths; one very steep descent. Good footwear required

Distance/time: 8 kilometres/ 5 miles. Allow 2 – 2½ hours

Start: Conwy town car park outside the town walls in Llanrwst Road (OR Morfa Conwy beach car park SH 761 786)

Grid ref: SH 781 773

Ordnance Survey map: OS Explorer OL17 Snowdon/Yr Wyddfa - *Conwy Valley/Dyffryn Conwy*

The Pub: The Erskine Arms, Rose Hill Street, Conwy LL32 8DL | 01492 593535 | www.erskinearms.co.uk

Walk outline: Beginning in the shadow of Conwy's famous castle, a climb onto the medieval town walls leads through the upper town and onto the lower slopes of Conwy Mountain with its stunning coastal views. A steep descent and a short road section take you out to the coast with a bracing walk along the dunes of Morfa Conwy, before turning into the Conwy Estuary and a return to Conwy.

The Erskine Arms is an interesting mix of Georgian coaching inn and 17th century sail-maker's cottage and has been beautifully renovated to produce a warm, inviting pub arranged on split levels. Local ales and excellent food make this the perfect end to a lovely coastal walk.

Britain's smallest house

▶ The Erskine Arms at a glance

Open: Mon to Sat 11.30am – 11pm | Sun 11.30am – 10.30pm
Brewery/company: Stange & Co Pubs
Ales and wine: Selection of local ales, plus extensive wine list
Food: Daily 12 noon – 9pm. Delicious menu of homemade pub classics along with seasonal specials. Selection of roasts served on Sundays
Outside: Secluded courtyard perfect to trap the summer sun and to keep away the cooler autumn winds
Children & dogs: Children's menu and highchairs available. Changing facilities. Dogs are welcome in the bar area and courtyard

The Walk

1. Head towards the **subway** at the back of the car park (which leads under the railway and gives access to the town). Immediately before the subway, take the rising road on the left signed to '**Tŵr Llewelyn**'. The road leads up beside the railway and through an **archway** in the **town walls**. Turn right immediately and climb the **spiral stairway** up onto the walls.

The town walls are some of the best preserved medieval walls in Europe. They were built, along with the castle, by Edward I in 1283 following his conquest of Wales.

The walls can be walked for almost three quarters of their length. The first section is along a wooden walkway, then, after the first **corner tower**, the original stone walkway continues to the **Upper Gate**, where there is another **spiral stairway**. Descend the stairway, turn right through the walls and bear left along the road.

2. Ignore a left (St Agnes Road), continuing ahead. Take the fourth turning on the right into **Cadnant Park**. Follow the road, which soon descends gradually before swinging right. Immediately after this, turn left into '**Mountain Road**'. Follow the road as it swings left, then rises. Ignoring a right, continue on the rising road and where it forks at the end of the tarmac, bear right up to a stile. Cross the stile and follow the clear footpath ahead onto **Conwy Mountain**.

The well worn path rises gradually through the trees. Shortly after you emerge from the woods, the path levels by a distinct flat rock. Turn right here and walk out to an impressive

© Crown copyright and/or database right. All rights reserved. Licence number 100047867

Walk 2 – **The Erskine Arms**, Conwy ♦ 17

"One of the most impressive walled circuits in Europe"

viewpoint overlooking Conwy and the river mouth.

The superb view from here takes in the wide sweep of Conwy Bay, from the east coast of Anglesey and Puffin Island to the Great Orme and Llandudno. You can see almost the entire route from here.

3. Turn around with your back to the estuary and bear right onto a grassy path. In about 50 metres turn right onto a narrow path that cuts diagonally down the steep slopes (**care needed**) towards the main road below. Partway down the slope, turn right again and head more steeply down towards a stile visible below.

Cross the stile and the road opposite **'Bryn Morfa' caravan park** entrance and turn left along the road. Cross the **A55** and take the first left signed to **'Aberconwy Resort & Spa'**.

Walk past the Spa entrance and immediately before the **beach car park** turn sharp right onto the coastal path. The path follows the top of the **sand dunes** between the **golf course** and the beach with views out over the river mouth to the Great Orme.

The amazing panorama across Afon Conwy to the Great Orme from Conwy Mountain

4. At the far end of the golf course, the dunes curve rightwards into the mouth of **Afon Conwy**. Pass through the car park and slipway and continue ahead on a footpath to reach **Conwy Quays Marina** on the right.

Turn right and follow the path beside the marina. Turn left along the path between the marina and the houses on the waterfront. Before you reach the far end, look for the signed **Wales Coast Path** directing you right between the houses. Take the left fork in a few metres keeping ahead to a road T-junction (**Telford Close**). Turn left, then first right to cross over the A55.

In around 200 metres turn left immediately before the **school** onto a tarmaced footpath. This follows the edge of the **estuary** into Conwy.

5. At the end of the path turn left through the **town walls** and walk along the **waterfront** passing the famous **smallest house in Wales**.

Immediately after the **Liverpool Arms**, turn right through **Lower Gate** in the walls and walk up **High Street** keeping ahead at the crossroads.

You will pass Aberconwy House on the left and Plas Mawr on the right part way up the High Street — both fine period houses.

6. At the top of the rise in the centre of the town, a left turn along **Church Street** will take you to the **Erskine Arms**.

Leave the Erskine Arms by the main entrance and turn left along **Rose Hill Street**. Cross the road after the **Visitor Centre**, take the path through the gatehouse and down the steps. Turn right through the subway to return to the car park to complete the walk. ♦

Plas Mawr
Plas Mawr, meaning the 'Great Hall', was built between 1576 and 1585 by Robert Wynn, an influential and prosperous Welsh merchant. It is said to be the best preserved Elizabethan town house to be found anywhere in Britain. The house is noted for both the quality and quantity of ornamental plasterwork which proclaimed Wynn's status and wealth. Plas Mawr is held in the care of Cadw and is open to the public. ***www.cadw.gov.wales***

The Ship Inn enjoys a sheltered location overlooking Red Wharf Bay

Anglesey/Ynys Môn

walk 3

Ship Inn
Red Wharf Bay

What to expect:
A mainly tidal section of the Wales Coast Path around the bay. Some muddy sections

Distance/time: 11.5 kilometres / 7 miles. Allow 4 hours
Start: Beach car park, Llandonna where there are toilets and seasonal café
Grid ref: SH 568 806
Ordnance Survey map: Explorer 263, Anglesey East, *Beaumaris, Amlwch & Menai Bridge*
The Pub: The Ship Inn, Red Wharf Bay, Pentraeth LL75 8RJ
01248 852568 | www.shipinnredwharfbay.co.uk

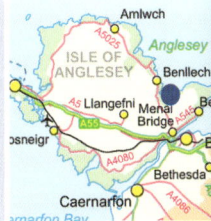

Walk outline: This is a straightforward walk around the edge of Red Wharf Bay and back following the Wales Coast Path. Sections can be muddy and there are tidal implications, although high tide alternatives are available. To be safe, avoid walking this route one hour each side of high tide.

The Ship Inn is a quaint, family-friendly, wood-beamed pub in a superb position overlooking the broad, tidal sands of Red Wharf Bay. Sheltered by the hill at its back, the pub and its outdoor tables catch the morning and afternoon sun. All this makes it the perfect place to enjoy the pub's hearty food, well-kept real ales and excellent choice of whiskies.

Summer on the patio

▶ The Ship Inn at a glance

Open: Daily. Monday – Thursday, 12 noon – 8pm; Friday – Saturday, 12 noon – 9pm; Sunday, 12 noon – 8pm
Brewery/company: Freehouse. Run by the Kenneally family since 1971
Ales and wine: Good selection of real ales including Kenneally's Bitter from Conwy Brewery, Dave's Hoppy Beer, and Somerby Apple Cider
Food: Served daily. Classic pub food and daily specials board, including seafood, 'dragon pie' and ever-popular chowder.
Outside: Sheltered tables at the front of the pub overlooking the bay
Children & dogs: Both welcome, large family room

The Walk

1. Leaving the **car park** turn left and walk along the lane. Where the road bends sharp left, turn right, leaving the lane to cross a small **footbridge**. Follow the path ahead behind the dunes and along the edge of open saltmarsh. Boardwalks carry the path over the wettest sections.

At steps, go up onto a **large stone-built seawall**. This is 0.5 kilometre/¼ mile long and gives a good, raised view across the saltmarsh meadows.

2. After the sea wall, pass the entrance to a lane on the left. Continue ahead at the head of the saltmarsh to reach the tidal parking area at **Pentraeth beach**.

From the beach car park cross the bridge over **Afon Nodwydd** and follow the **tidal access track** that soon loses itself amongst the sandy marshes.

The edge of the bay is a mixture of sand, mud and saltmarsh. After a small stone footbridge a lane leads down onto the marsh and a new footpath has been constructed tight against the marsh edge.

3. At the next group of houses ('**Porth Llôngdy Uchaf**') bear left up a tarmac road that comes down onto the marsh and after about 100 metres, look for the signed coastal footpath on the right (kissing gate). Follow this enclosed footpath along a wooded bank above the marsh to emerge in Red Wharf Bay beside the **Ship Inn**.

To return, retrace your route back around the marsh edge to the **Pentraeth beach car park**. From here you can either continue along the outward route, OR take the inland route described below.

4. Turn right at the T-junction after **Afon Nodwydd** and take the first lane on the left signed for the coast path. At the end of the lane bear right at a fork along an unmade access road. At a junction by houses, take the track on the left to '**Gallty-môr**'.

The boardwalk section at Llandonna beach

In around 500 metres, and immediately after the gateway to '**Tan y Mynydd**', take the footpath signed for the coast path on the right. The footpath heads up through the woods, soon turning left and descending to a kissing gate. Through the gate, the path continues ahead along the edge of woods. Pass **two cottages** on the left and a little further on cross a ladder stile over the wall on the right. Turn left here continuing along the edge of woods soon passing above a **farm** on the left. The path curves left shortly to join the farm access road. Follow this down to the lane and turn left down to the beach. Turn right and retrace the outward route to compete the walk. ♦

Land Rover Defender testing ground

The Land Rover Defender was, and is, one of the most successful road vehicles of all time — over two million were made before production ceased in January 2016. The Defender was designed by mechanical engineer Maurice Wilks who is said to have made the first ever sketch of his ideas on a visit to the beach here with his brother. Before this iconic vehicle went into production in 1948, the prototypes were tested on the sands in Red Wharf Bay.

Enjoying a drink on the White Eagle's sunny timber deck

Anglesey/Ynys Môn

The White Eagle
Rhoscolyn

walk 4

What to expect:
Good coastal path, narrow in places. Farmland paths sometimes with cattle

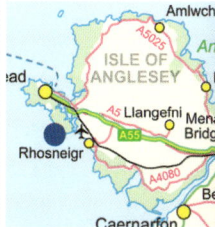

Distance/Time: 8.5 kilometres/ 5¼ miles. Allow 3 hours
Start: A few cars can be parked beside Saint Gwenfaen's Church, Rhoscolyn. Alternatively, there is a small beach car park at the end of the lane at Borthwen (point 3. on the map)
Grid Ref: SH 269 758
Ordnance Survey Map: Explorer 262 Anglesey West: *Holyhead/Caergybi*
The Pub: The White Eagle, Rhoscolyn, Holyhead LL65 2NJ
01407 860267 | www.white-eagle.co.uk

Walk outline: A quiet lane and farmland paths lead down to the coast to join the Wales Coast Path, where you have the option of a detour to view the natural sea arch of Bwa Gwyn. The route then follows a rugged section of coast to Borthwen at Rhoscolyn, followed by open coastal heath, before a return along a quiet lane and field paths.

Stylishly modernised by the philanthropist Timpson family in 2007, The White Eagle, *with its picture windows and timber patio, overlooks the rugged Anglesey coast at Rhoscolyn. This friendly, atmospheric gastro pub has a good range of real and guest ales, quality wines, and a superb menu that makes clever use of both seasonal and local produce.*

Looking out to the patio

▶ The White Eagle at a glance
Open: Daily from 12 noon
Brewery/company: Freehouse
Ales and wine: Great selection of real ales and ciders including Eagle IPA, West Coast Pale Ale, White Eagle lager; good choice of wines
Food: Superb seasonal menu featuring home-made British dishes, using local meat, vegetables and seafood. Food served daily, 12 noon - 8pm, and 12 noon - 9pm on Friday and Saturday
Accommodation: 'The Nest', a 4 bedroom apartment
Outside: Large, elevated timber patio and garden with great views
Children & dogs: Children and dogs both welcome

The coast path winds through heather and gorse at Rhoscolyn

The Walk

1. Follow the lane past the **church**. After **Lodge Bach** on the left, the lane becomes a farm track. The track continues to a farm surrounded by a high walled farmyard. Immediately before this, look for a kissing gate and signed footpath on the right. The right of way heads down a small field, goes through a footgate in the bottom corner, then turns left around the farm.

At the far side of the farm, turn right and follow a footpath between **ruined stone walls** down to join the coast path.

(To visit **Bwa Gwyn sea arch** turn right here but return to this point to continue the walk.)

2. Turn left through a kissing gate and follow the coast path keeps which close to a well-built **stone wall** on the left with cliffs to the right all the way to Rhoscolyn Head. Take care near several deep inlets.

Stay beside the wall as it curves left after **Rhoscolyn Head** and take care on the final section before the kissing gate where the gap between the wall and the cliffs on the right becomes much narrower! The path is visible now as it crosses open ground aiming directly for the **Coastguard Lookout** and passing Saint Gwenfaen's Well (see box on p29).

The Coastguard Lookout enjoys a magnificent panorama across much of the west coast of Anglesey and Holy Island.

Pass to the left of the Coastguard Lookout, following the signed coast path directly down sloping grazing fields (distant small square tower ahead). After a kissing gate, cross the access road to **The Point** and continue ahead on a wall-enclosed path eventually between gardens, and finally turning right across a lawn to reach the road by **stone gate posts** at 'Bryn Eithin'.

Follow the access road left between houses and past a tiny cove on the right to reach **Borthwen**—the main beach at Rhoscolyn. A tidal road crosses the beach and can be walked most of the time but if the water is too high, look for steps on the left immediatley before a concrete sea wall that lead up to a path along the top of the wall, rejoining the beach by the entrance to the **car park**.

3. Turn left through the car park (public toilets) and continue along the lane. At the first bend turn right onto the signed coast path. Follow the path along the back of the bay. At a fork, keep ahead (right) and follow the path to join a track leading to houses on the right ('Cil Bwch'). Walk left along the track and at a T-junction turn right. Pass between

© Crown copyright and/or database right. All rights reserved. Licence number 100047867

The natural sea arch of Bwa Gwyn (meaning 'white arch')

the houses and almost at the end of the track (beside 'Borth Esgob') go through the kissing gate ahead onto the **open coastal heath**. Follow the well-defined path ahead marked by yellow-topped posts.

Dropping down into the tiny shingle cove of **Porth Gorslwyn**, go over three small **sleeper bridges**, head up through gorse and cross a field to a kissing gate. Follow the well-defined path around another headland of coastal heath all the way to **Silver Bay**.

4. Turn right down the **access ramp** onto the beach. Bear left along the sand and in about 250 metres, turn left up **timber steps** into a small **pine wood**. Follow a fenced path through the trees ahead.

Beyond the wood, keep ahead through a kissing gate and along a **wooden boardwalk** to a kissing gate into a field. Go through the gate and head across the field towards the buildings of **Bryn-y-bar**. Pass to the right of the buildings to join the access track. Follow the track ahead.

The track becomes a tarmac lane. Continue along the lane keeping right at a fork. Shortly after '**Ty Lôn**' on the left, look for a metal kissing gate also on the left adjacent to the access road to '**Coedan**'.

5. Go through the gate and ahead through a small field to the kissing gate in the far corner. This leads onto a wooded path beside a **campsite**, then cuts through an area of scrub to enter fields again. Go ahead through two fields to reach an access road by **cottages**. Walk down the access road to the lane and turn right. The **White Eagle** is on the left as you walk along the lane. To return to the start point, turn left at the end of the lane. ♦

Holy Well

The small stone enclosure on the clifftop near Rhoscolyn Head is Saint Gwenfaen's Well: the remains of a medieval healing well. It has stone steps, corner seats and may have originally been roofed. During the Middle Ages, like so many other sites, it became a place of pilgrimage — a gift of two white quartz pebbles thrown into the pool were believed to cure mental health problems.

The Oystercatcher is set on the edge of extensive dunes

Anglesey/Ynys Môn

The Oystercatcher
Rhosneigr

walk 5

What to expect:
Easy walking on cliff-top Coast Path, inland paths and farm tracks

Distance/time: 8 kilometres/ 5 miles. Allow 2½ hours
Start: On the outskirts of Rhosneigr, opposite The Oystercatcher pub there is parking available in a large roadside lay-by close to reed-fringed Llyn Maelog
Grid ref: SH 325 726
Ordnance Survey map: Explorer 262 Anglesey West: *Holyhead/Caergybi*
The Pub: The Oystercatcher, Maelog Lake, Rhosneigr LL64 5JP | 01407 812 829 | www.oystercatcheranglesey.co.uk

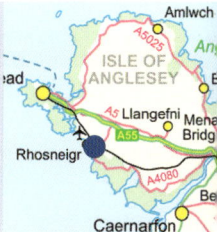

Walk outline: This walk combines a circuit of an attractive coastal lake with the popular watersports beach at Rhosneigr. It also visits the spectacular headland setting of the Neolithic burial chamber known as Barclodiad y Gawres, with a return along the Wales Coast Path to finish at the distinctive modern Oystercatcher pub.

Set amongst Rhosneigr's extensive sand dunes and just a stone's throw from one of Anglesey's prime surfing beaches, The Oystercatcher's *clean minimalist lines are the creation of the Timpson family (better known for their shoe repair business). The building was delivered and assembled by Huf Haus, a German company famous for their modern, eco-friendly designs, in 2009.*

The Oystercatcher

▶ The Oystercatcher at a glance

Open: Daily 10am - 11pm
Brewery/company: Freehouse
Ales and wine: Draught real ales from Great Orme, Conwy and Weetwood breweries plus guest and bottled beers. Excellent selection of wines
Food: Available during opening hours. Good selection of dishes showcasing the pub's relationship with local farms and producers
Outside: Extensive area of outside seating as well as a large first floor balcony with stunning views across the sand dunes
Children & dogs: Both welcome

The Walk

1. From the parking area and facing the pub, turn left along the road. A few metres after the **bridge** turn left down an **unmade access road** marked 'Private Road'. Pass several houses on the right and bear left onto a clear footpath which follows the edge of **Llyn Maelog**. At the head of the lake cross a small **footbridge** and keep left around the shore edge.

Llyn Maelog was originally a tidal inlet of the sea which has been dammed and turned into a freshwater pool by the sand dunes of Tywyn Llyn. Its formation is similar to that of Llyn Coron near Aberffraw which has also been isolated from the sea by wind blown sand forming the massive dunes of Tywyn Aberffraw. The lake is fairly shallow for its size being rarely more than seven feet deep and is often used for canoeing and windsurfing.

The reed-fringed shore gives excellent cover to birds; nesting species include great crested grebe, little grebe, coot, moorhen, tufted duck and mallard.

The path around the lake is clear, well used and passes a **caravan site** before the final section along an all user **board walk**.

© Crown copyright and/or database right. All rights reserved. Licence number 100047867

2. At the road cross diagonally leftwards and walk down the road opposite ('**Lakeside Estate**'). Almost immediately, turn left onto a **gravel access road** between houses. Where this swings right into 'Private' grounds, keep ahead

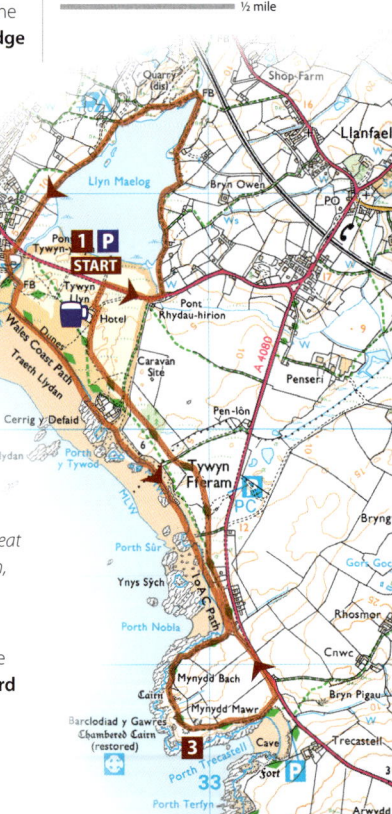

Traeth Llydan beach at Rhosneigr

on a sandy track. Before the dunes, bear left off the track through a picnic area and cross a small footbridge over a stream. Turn right immediately and walk down onto the beach beside the stream (**Traeth Llydan**). Turn left along the beach.

Rhosneigr has been a popular resort since the closing years of the nineteenth century when a small station on the Holyhead railway line gave visitors access to what would otherwise have been a remote corner of the island. Prior to this, Rhosneigr was a tiny settlement making its living from fishing.

The name Rhosneigr is thought to be derived from 'Yneigr' 'a maiden' and 'rhos' meaning 'moor'—its English translation would thus be 'Moor of the Maid'.

The word 'Rhos' appears in many Welsh place names and moors are still a familiar part of the Welsh landscape. In Rhosneigr's case the 'moor' referred to is undoubtedly the large area of dunes to the north of the village known as Tywyn Trewan. Centuries of dune formation have provided a defence from the sea and created an ideal location for the RAF airbase which now occupies the western half of the common.

The Oystercatcher enjoys an enviable position among the coastal dunes

(**Alternatively, for Rhosneigr village** where there are shops, pubs and cafés, turn right along the road. In the centre of the village there is a post office and convenience store on the crossroads.

Turn left along **High Street**. This eventually curves left and becomes '**Lôn Traeth Llydan**', with houses on the left, then on both sides. At a distinct left turn take the beach access road straight ahead which takes you down onto **Traeth Llydan**, signed for the coastal path.)

Walk along two large stretches of sand passing the houses at **Cerrig y Defaid** and one smaller cove (**Porth Nobola**), separated by low rocks, before joining the **coastal footpath** which skirts the grassy headland of **Mynydd Mawr**.

At the end of the headland is one of the most famous prehistoric monuments on the island—Barclodiad y Gawres. A fine burial chamber from the Neolithic period and in one of the most magnificent settings, it was 'restored' following excavation in the 1950s.

3. Continue round into **Porth Trecastell** (Cable Bay). Walk through the **beach car park** and turn left along the road. Around 400 metres on, look for the Coast Path sign on the left near a parking area. Just before the beach (**Porth Nobola** again) the path forks; keep right, passing a **small cottage** and follow the path along the top of the dunes to pass through a beach car park. Continue on the **signed coast path** which continues across dunes towards a group of **large houses** at **Cerrig y Defaid**. Cross the gravel access road and follow the signed coast path ahead and beneath overhead cables to eventually reach **The Oystercatcher** to complete the walk. ♦

Barclodiad y Gawres

The curious name Barclodiad y Gawres translates as 'The Giantess's Apronful' and refers to the heaped stones that once formed the original burial mound. Today, an iron gated modern entrance leads into a concrete-capped inner chamber featuring several large decorated stones. Similar massive stones decorated with spirals, zig-zags and lozenges are found in Neolithic tombs in the Boyne Valley, across the sea in Ireland.

The Tŷ Coch is the archetypal 'pub on the beach'

Llŷn Peninsula/Pen Llŷn

Tŷ Coch Inn
Porth Dinllaen

walk 6

What to expect:
Easy walking on filed paths and well-used coastal path

Distance/Time: 12 kilometres/ 7½ miles. Allow 5-6 hours
Start: Large National Trust car park (fee payable) at the end of 'Lon Golf' (Golf Lane) in Morfa Nefyn
Grid Ref: SH 282 407
Ordnance Survey Map: Explorer 253 Llŷn Peninsula West: *Pwllheli, Abersoch & Aberdaron*
The Pub: Ty Coch Inn, Porth Dinllaen, Nefyn LL53 | 01758 720498 www.tycoch.co.uk

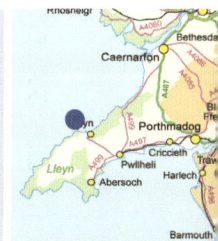

Walk outline: Easy walking across the golf course and farmland to join the Wales Coast Path. This is then followed back around the edge of the golf course and the headland of Trwyn Porth Dinllaen to the unique hamlet of Porth Dinllaen where you will find the lovely Tŷ Coch pub on the beach. An easy stroll along the beach completes the walk.

A traditional tavern on the shore in the tiny National Trust owned hamlet of Porth Dinllaen, with local real ale and pub food. Access to the pub is on foot only with a 20 minute walk across the golf course or along the beach at low tide. Interesting local maritime memorabilia and photographs adorn the walls and beams, and there is ample outside seating.

Window above the beach

▶ The Tŷ Coch at a glance

Open: Open only when the weather is good. Reduced opening at low season and closed on Sundays; worth calling for opening times
Brewery/company: Free house
Real ales: Range of local beers and ciders
Food: Some hot food and pasties, plus sandwiches, coffee, ice creams
Accommodation: The pub owns two holiday rentals in Porth Dinllaen, a flat and a cottage
Outside: Plenty of outdoor tables, or sit on the sea wall or beach
Children & dogs: Children and dogs welcome

The Walk

1. Turn right out of the car park and follow the road to the **golf club** and '**RNLI House**'. Go through the gate onto the golf course and follow the rough, surfaced track across the golf course.

Part way along the track — around 400 metres or so — you will see the signed footpath on the left (beside a large 'agricultural' type buliding). Turn left here following the right of way across the golf course. You should be able to see the footpath sign at the far side of the fairway.

2. Turn left behind the teeing off area as signed and follow the right of way soon enclosed between high hedges. The footpath becomes a farm access road after a campsite on the right.

As you approach **Porth Dinllaen Farm** keep ahead at a fork to reach a T-junction.

© Crown copyright and/or database right. All rights reserved. Licence number 100047867

Turn right here heading towards the farm initially, then bear left following a farm track to the left of the farmhouse. Follow this down through gates to cross a stream by a farm bridge at the bottom of the field. Beyond a gate, after the bridge,

Walk 6 – **Tŷ Coch**, Porth Dinllaen ♦ 39

Aerial view of Porth Dinllaen and Trwyn Porth Dinllaen

the right of way swings right through an open field, through another gate and second stream.

Keep left in the next field and walk along the field edge towards a large **farmhouse**. Go right in the field corner and keep beside the hedge. Go through the kissing gate in the field corner and follow the right of way along a raised bank towards **farm outbuildings**.

At the end of the bank drop down into a farmyard and bear right beside large farm buildings. Follow a farm track ahead, which soon becomes a footpath enclosed between hedges. Follow this all the way down to the coast where you join the Wales Coast Path above a **small cove**.

3. Turn right and follow the coast path. At **Aber Geirch** — a small rocky bay with a pipeline running into the water — the coast path drops down to cross a stream by a footbridge before climbing back onto the low rocky cliffs to continue around the **golf course** again.

Continue around the edge of the golf course until you near the point close to where you crossed the course on

Cottages and the Tŷ Coch pub at Porth Dinllaen

the outward route. Don't cut across the fairway, instead continue around the edge of the small bay of **Borth Wen**. This leads out onto the finger-like headland of **Trwyn Porth Dinllaen**.

Continue to the **old coastguard lookout** almost at the end of the headland. The coast path passes to the right of the lookout and continues above tidal rocks *where Atlantic grey seals can often be seen basking at low tide.*

The path passes above the **Lifeboat Station** heading down the concrete ramp, past a tiny sandy beach, then continues just above the high tideline. As you enter **Porth Dinllaen** the path passes between cottages and emerges on the beach close to the **Tŷ Coch**.

It is hard to believe, as you walk through this tiny hamlet, that in the eighteenth and early nineteenth centuries it was set to become one of the busiest sea ports in North Wales and for a time even rivalled Holyhead as the ferry port for Ireland.

One of North Wales' major communication obstacles had been removed with the building of Alexander Maddocks' embankment across Afon Glaslyn at Porthmadog, placing Porth Dinllaen conveniently at the end of an excellent coach road. The hamlet braced itself for great things, but Holyhead won the day!

Walk 6 – **Tŷ Coch**, Porth Dinllaen

It was a lucky escape — this lovely spot has remained largely undisturbed ever since.

4. To complete the walk you can either follow the road up behind the pub and back across the golf course, or, if the tide allows, walk back along the beach and turn right up the road access at **Morfa Nefyn**. The car park access is part way up the road on the right. ♦

Pub on the beach!

The Tŷ Coch Inn at Porth Dinllaen started life as the vicarage for the local church at Edern. Built in 1823 of red bricks brought in as ballast from Holland, it was soon referred to locally as the Red House. But when a new vicarage was built beside the church, the house became one of four pubs on the beach serving the busy local shipbuilding industry.

The Tŷ Newydd features a terrace overhanging the beach

Llŷn Peninsula/Pen Llŷn

Tŷ Newydd
Aberdaron

walk 7

What to expect:
Good, well used coast and field paths. Some stretches along quiet lanes

Distance/Time: 9.5 kilometres / 6 miles. Allow 2-3 hours
Start: Parking is limited to a large National Trust pay and display car park in the centre of Aberdaron
Grid Ref: SH 172 264
Ordnance Survey Map: Explorer 253 Llŷn Peninsula West: *Pwllheli, Abersoch & Aberdaron*
The Pub: Gwesty Ty Newydd, Aberdaron LL53 8BE | 01758 760207
www.gwesty-tynewydd.co.uk

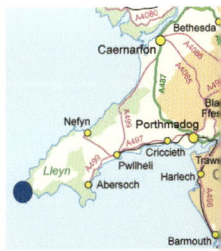

Walk outline: From Aberdaron, the route follows a superb section of the Wales Coast Path to the western tip of Llŷn with stunning views to the enigmatic isle of Bardsey. A return to Aberdaron is made by gentle inland lanes and field paths.

A friendly, comfortable four star hotel in the heart of Aberdaron overlooking the sandy beach and offshore islands. There is a spacious bar and dining room with home-made and locally sourced food including Bardsey-caught crab and lobster, as well as local beers. Outdoor tables on the terrace above the beach give the Tŷ Newydd a unique feel. Recommended in the Good Beer Guide.

Balcony with a view

▶ **Tŷ Newydd at a glance**

Open: Daily, 11am – midnight
Brewery/company: Freehouse
Real ales: Purple Moose Calon Lan plus changing local cask ales
Food: Open for morning coffee, lunch, afternoon tea, evening meals. Lunch 12 noon - 2.30pm. Evening meals 6.00 - 8.30pm; children's menu.
Rooms: 11 Bedrooms - all en-suite with sea view
Outside: Elevated terrace with tables
Children & dogs: Children very welcome; dogs in yellow room and terrace, but not in bar or restaurant

Sunrise at Aberdaron

The Walk

1. Turn left out of the car park, then left again along the lane signed to '**Porthor, Whistling Sand**'. The lane rises steeply out of Aberdaron and you soon have a wide view out across the village to the beach and bay.

Aberdaron was traditionally the end of the 'Saint's Road' taken by pilgrims en-route to Bardsey during the Middle Ages. An indication of the difficulty of the journey in those days is given by the fact that three pilgrimages to Bardsey were said to equal one to Rome.

At the top of the rise, immediately after an access ramp, take the signed coastal path on the left into the National Trust land at '**Porth Simdde**'. A fenced footpath heads along the edge of fields overlooking the bay.

Descend steps into a small valley (Porth Simdde), cross the **footbridge** and climb steps up to the cliff-top coast path.

Turn left and follow the coastal path to **Porth Meudwy**, also known as 'Fisherman's Cove', where **steps** lead down into the tiny inlet.

Porth Meudwy is a tiny rocky cove tucked into the cliffs. For centuries, it has been the embarkation point for boats to Bardsey.

2. Cross the **footbridge** ahead and climb the steps to reach the clifftop coastal path again. The way ahead is straightforward now, a good, well-used footpath hugging the top of the cliffs on the outside edge of fenced fields on the right.

3. In just under two kilometres, around a mile, the path turns right rising up through more open rough grazing land. Soon Bardsey comes into view and a little further on the cairn marking the high point of **Pen y Cil** — the southernmost tip of Uwchmynydd — is reached.

Go through two kissing gates separated by a small field on the left and into a larger field close to the deep rocky inlet of **Parwyd**. Keep left along the field edge and go through a gate in the far corner into the rough grazing land of **Mynydd Bychestyn**.

The coast path heads initially down towards the sea with Bardsey directly ahead and following white-tipped posts, before veering right above the sea cliffs.

4. A kissing gate eventually leads into a narrower grazing field with walled fields on the right. Continue ahead, the path still marked by white-tipped posts, to

© Crown copyright and/or database right. All rights reserved. Licence number 100047867

Bardsey was the spiritual goal of pilgrims throughout the Middle Ages

reach a footgate above the rocky cove of **Porth Felen** where seals can often be seen. Through the gate, the path heads diagonally-left up to a saddle on the shoulder of **Mynydd y Gwyddel**. From here the coast path contours around the hillside with good views across to Bardsey.

The path curves into a shallow valley with a stream that is often dry in the summer. Bear right off the coastal path here up beside the stream to eventually reach a **lane**. Bear right and walk along the lane.

5. In around 1 kilometre/½ mile, where the lane turns left (by '**Pen Bryn Bach**'), bear right down a farm access road. The right of way passes the **farm** on the right and enters a field. Keep to the left-hand edge and take a direct line through following fields to join the driveway to a **cottage** on the left. Bear right down the drive to the lane and turn right.

In about 25 metres take the signed footpath on the left which follows a **raised bank** between fields to reach another lane.

Turn left along the lane and in about 400 metres, after a right-hand bend, you reach the National Trust land at '**Cwrt**'. Turn sharp right onto the rough road, then bear left almost immediately onto a farm track. This rises to a large

Walk 8 – **Tŷ Newydd**, Aberdaron ♦ 47

field. Bear half-right across the field, then go through a gateway on the left. Rise up the bank and bear right onto a descending path to eventually join a track in the bottom of a small valley.

Bear left along the track to **Porth Meudwy**. Take the coast path left up the steps and retrace the outward route back to **Aberdaron** to complete the walk. ♦

'Port of the Hermits'

The sheltered cove of Porth Meudwy, near Aberdaron, was the traditional embarkation point for pilgrims crossing to Bardsey, or Ynys Enlli. During bad weather the island can be cut off for weeks, and pilgrims often had to wait patiently in Aberdaron. The pilgrimage to Bardsey was popular throughout the Middle Ages. Today, modern fast boats still leave Porth Meudwy for Bardsey.
For details, see: www.bardseyboattrips.com

The Sun has a spacious and sunny beer garden

Llŷn Peninsula/Pen Llŷn

walk 8

The Sun/Tafarn Yr Haul
Llanengan

What to expect:
Good coastal path for much of the time. Some farmland paths and occasional lanes too

Distance/time: 12 kilometres/ 7½ miles. Allow 3-4 hours

Start: Free parking in a small beach car park at Pentowyn near the southeastern end of Hell's Mouth near the village of Llanengan

Grid ref: SH 248 266

Ordnance Survey Map: Explorer 253 Llŷn Peninsula West: *Pwllheli, Abersoch & Aberdaron*

The Pub: The Sun/Tafarn Yr Haul, Llanengan, Pwllheli, Gwynedd LL53 7LG | 01758 712660 | www.thesunllanengan.co.uk

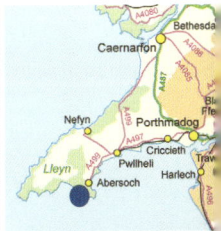

Walk outline: Beginning on the storm beach at Hell's Mouth (Porth Neigwl), this route follows the Wales Coast Path up onto the headland of Mynydd Cilan — a spectacular stretch of heath-covered sea cliff between Hell's Mouth and Abersoch now designated a Special Protection Area. The walking is straightforward all the way to Porth Ceiriad with a return through farmland and quiet lanes.

The Sun Inn is a traditional, Cask Marque-winning, real ale country pub popular with locals and visitors alike. Families, walkers and dogs are all welcome. There is plenty of outdoor space for eating and drinking as well as a large, comfortable bar, lounge and games area.

The Sun, Llanengan

▶ The Sun at a glance

Open: Daily 12 noon – 11pm
Brewery/company: Robinsons
Ales and wine: Robinsons real ales as well as a wide selection of lagers, wines, spirits and cider, tea, coffee and soft drinks
Food: Classic pub lunches 12 noon - 2pm; evening meals with Specials board, vegetarian options, local seafood 6 - 9pm
Outside: Spacious and sunny beer garden
Children & dogs: Both welcome

The Walk

1. From the car park at **Pentowyn**, take the path down towards the beach. Immediately before the beach, turn left onto the coast path which follows the top of the dunes. Continue to the far end of the bay.

Go through the kissing gate at the end of the beach and walk ahead up the field edge to two kissing gates. Go through the right-hand gate and walk up beside the fence on the left. Cross a **wooden footbridge** and continue high above the bay with increasingly spectacular views. Go through a kissing gate tight below a line of low cliffs and follow the path beside the rocks to a second kissing gate. Go through the gate and out onto the open heath of **Mynydd Cilan**. The path rises gently over the heather-covered slopes indicated by waymarker posts.

2. At a path T-junction, turn right onto a broad grassy path which heads off across the common. Soon, the path passes beside small fields on the left to reach an **Ordnance Survey triangulation pillar**.

There are wide views from here across Hell's Mouth to Mynydd Rhiw and distant Bardsey at the extreme

© Crown copyright and/or database right. All rights reserved. Licence number 100047867

Approaching Porth Ceiriad on the Wales Coast Path

western end of Llŷn. To the southeast there are distant views to the mountains of Snowdonia including Cadair Idris and the skyline of the Rhinog hills.

Continue on the broad path as it curves left around the headland. Stay on the open grass footpath following the waymarkers until directed left at the southern tip of the headland on **Trwyn Cilan**. This is about 1.25 kilometres/¾ mile from the triangulation pillar.

3. The path now makes its way between gorse bushes and bracken until you reach fields enclosed by walls and fences ahead. Turn right here and walk down beside the wall and fence as signed. Near the cliff edge, go through the kissing gate ahead (ignore a path to the left) and walk down beside the fence with the cliff edge close by on the right. *Take care:* the path between the fence and the cliff edge is not very wide here.

4. At the end of the cliffs — **Trwyn Llech-y-doll** — the path turns left into the wide sweep of **Porth Ceiriad**. A little further on the path crosses a footbridge over a stream before rising steeply up the bank.

At the top of the rise ignore the signed

On the Wales Coast Path above Trwyn Llech-y-doll

footpath on the left signed to '**Muriau**', keeping ahead on the coast path. The path follows the upper edge of steep grassy slopes that give wide views across Porth Ceiriad.

After kissing gates, the coast path is enclosed on both sides by fences and following it is straightforward all the way to a small car park immediately above **Porth Ceiriad** beach.

5. At the end of the car park, go through a kissing gate and turn left off the coast path rising up the bank to a footpath T-junction. Turn left and follow the path up to join the **Nant-y-big Caravan and Campsite** access road.

Head right along the road and continue to the T-junction at the end.

6. Turn right along the lane and in less than 100 metres look for a signed footpath on the left. This heads along a grassy drive towards a small **cottage**. Turn left along the drive and just before the cottage go right through a small footgate. Turn left along the field edge towards a **Bryn Celyn Isaf farm**.

Enter the farmyard and bear left along a farm track between fields. After a **cattle grid** the track enters open fields. Where it swings to the right, go ahead down the bank (left slightly) to eventually join another track. Go right down towards a cottage. Immediately before the cottage turn right along a farm track. At the end of the field go through a kissing gate on the left and walk down to cross a **foobridge** in the field corner. Go ahead now following a farm track.

Pass **Tan Ralt Farm** and continue to the lane where a right turn will take you to the **The Sun**.

From The Sun return along the lane to the car park to complete the walk. ♦

Dolphins and porpoise

Trwyn Cilan (pronounced True-in Killan) is one of the distinctive headlands of the western tip of the Llŷn Peninsula. Bottlenose- and common dolphins and porpoise can often be seen feeding offshore, when the tide is right, as food is concentrated by the fierce currents. The headland's gorse- and heather clad lowland heath is an increasingly rare habitat that supports common lizards, adders, stonechats, wheatears and breeding choughs.

Enjoying outdoor eating at the Glyn y Weddw

Llŷn Peninsula/Pen Llŷn

Glyn y Weddw Arms
Llanbedrog

walk 9

What to expect:
Coast and woodland paths with some steep sections and wide views

Distance/time: 7 kilometres/ 4½ miles. Allow 2 hours
Start: Free parking for a few cars in a short dead end lane off the A499, a mile or so east of Llanbedrog
Grid ref: SH 340 327
Ordnance Survey Map: Explorer 253 Llŷn Peninsula West: *Pwllheli, Abersoch & Aberdaron*
The Pub: The Glyn y Weddw Arms, Llanbedrog, Pwllheli, LL53 7TH
01758-740212 | www.glynyweddw.com

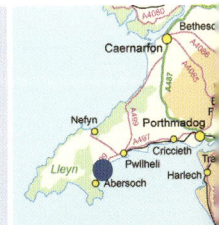

Walk outline: Starting at Carreg y Defaid to the east of Llanbedrog the coast path is followed to Llanbedrog before heading up through the grounds of Plas Glyn-y-Weddw and onto Mynydd Tir-cwmwd headland with its wide views. After a circuit of the headland, return to Llanbedrog where you will find the Glyn y Weddw Arms, before retracing the outward route.

The Glyn y Weddw Arms is a warm, friendly family pub popular with both locals and visitors. Families, walkers and dogs are all welcome. There is plenty of outdoor space for eating and drinking, including a heated patio area, as well as a large, comfortable lounge and bar.

Colourful beach huts

▶ The Glyn y Weddw Arms at a glance

Open: Daily 12 noon - 11pm
Brewery/company: Robinsons
Ales and wine: Robinsons real ales as well as a wide selection of lagers, wines, spirits and cider, tea, coffee and soft drinks
Food: Plenty of choice from pub classics to Sunday roast; locally sourced seasonal produce. Lunchtime snack and sandwiches available as well as children's menu. Food served daily 12 noon - 9pm
Outside: Tables in front of the pub; covered, heated patio and children's play area
Children & dogs: Both welcome

2. Turn right up the beach access road and opposite the car park entrance, go left into the grounds of **Plas Glyn-y-Weddw** gallery and tearooms.

Pass in front of the house and immediately before the car park take the signed coast path directly ahead. Pass the **John Andrews Theatre** and continue ahead on the gently rising woodland path.

After stone steps a footpath T-junction is reached. Turn left here going through a gap in the wall to follow a stone-faced path along the upper wooded hillside. Keep ahead where a steep path joins from the left to eventually reach the curious **Tin Man sculpture** on the left.

3. Continue ahead on the obvious, broad footpath — the signed and waymarked Wales Coast Path. This contours around the headland high above the sea with great views in all directions.

4. After you pass above **The Warren**, a large distinctive development of chalets on the Abersoch side of the headland, you reach an **obvious fork**. The Wales Coast Path keeps left, but our route parts company here keeping straight ahead where you will soon see a **cottage** ahead.

At the cottage join the access track and follow it ahead. The track eventually joins a tarmac lane. Keep left down the hill

The Walk

1. Walk down to the end of the lane to join the coast path and turn right. The path curves around the headland of **Carreg y Defaid** to eventually enter fields. Follow the path along the field edges and above the beach.

Where the field path ends, bear left down **steps** onto the beach and turn right along the sand. Pass the brightly coloured **beach huts** to reach the beach access road where there is a **café/bar** and **toilets**.

A gull's-eye view of Llanbedrog beach below Mynydd Tir-cwmwd headland

and shortly turn right along an access road immediately before '**Bronwydd**' — a cottage on the right. (The track passes behind the cottage.) After the last house continue ahead on a footpath into woods to reach a T-junction.

5. Turn left and in a few metres go through a gate to pass a cottage on the left. Keep ahead down the access track, then turn right through a kissing gate. After a second kissing gate, bear left through a small field above Llanbedrog. At the road turn right, then left at the T-junction. Walk up the lane to reach the pub on the left.

After the pub head back down the lane to the beach and retrace the outward route to complete the walk. ♦

Headland figure

High on the headland of Mynydd Tir-cwmwd, above Llanbedrog, is Llŷn's famous 'Tin Man'. The first sculpture on the headland was a wooden ship's figurehead erected in 1919 by the owner of nearby Plas Glyn y Weddw. It was later replaced by an iron figure by local sculptor, Simon van de Put. When that finally rusted away, the current 'Tin Man' was helicoptered in, in June 2002.

The Australia is a friendly, modern real ale pub

walk 10

Llŷn Peninsula/Pen Llŷn

Yr Awstralia/The Australia
Porthmadog

What to expect:
Good footpaths, cycle route, quiet lanes and the village of Portmeirion

Distance/time: 8 kilometres/ 5 miles. Allow 3 hours
Start: Pay and Display car park in Porthmadog (from the southern end of the High Street, turn into Madog Street then turn right)
Grid ref: SH 570 387
Ordnance Survey Map: OS Explorer OL 18 Snowdonia *Harlech, Porthmadog & Y Bala*
The Pub: The Australia/Yr Awstralia, 31 High St, Porthmadog LL49 9LR | 01766 515957 | www.purplemoose.co.uk

Walk outline: A pretty walk that leaves the town by the famous Cob embankment, from where there are spectacular views across the estuary to the mountains of Snowdonia. The route then heads up into farmland behind Portmeirion, with the option to explore the Italian Riviera-inspired village. The return journey is back along the Cob.

Supposedly named after a local ship, The Australia is an friendly, modern real ale pub in the popular harbour town of Porthmadog. It's also the brewery tap for the town's famous Purple Moose Brewery (or Mŵs Piws in Welsh). The pub showcases the brewery's excellent cask, keg and bottled beers, as well as serving traditional home-cooked pub food.

Ship pub sign

▶ Yr Awstralia at a glance
Open: Daily 12 noon - 11pm
Brewery/company: Purple Moose Brewery
Ales and wine: Brewery tap for Purple Moose's cask, keg and bottled beers. Welsh cider and cocktails
Food: Freshly-prepared, home made pub grub served all year round
Children & dogs: Both welcome
Outside: No beer garden or outside seating

The Walk

1. Leave the car park to pass a supermarket on the left. At the T-junction, turn left, then left again at the next T-junction by the **petrol station**. Cross the railway lines and the **bridge** over **Afon Glaslyn**. You'll see the **Harbour Station** for **Ffestiniog** and **Welsh Highland Railways** over to your right.

The Ffestiniog Railway was built in the 1830s to transport slate from the Ffestiniog mines to the recently built harbour at Porthmadog.

2. Beyond the last buildings on the left, pick up the combined **cycle and pedestrian walkway** to the left of the **A497** road and cross the broad **Afon Glaslyn** estuary.

The stone embankment, which now carries both the road and railway (known as The Cob – 'Y Cob'), was built as a sea wall in 1811 by William Alexander Madocks. This enabled him to reclaim a huge area of tidal sands and saltmarsh known at the time as Traeth Mawr (the 'Great Beach'). The port of Porthmadog and town of Tremadog were built on the reclaimed land.

On the far side of **The Cob**, after a parking layby and immediately before a lane rises on the opposite side of the road, cross over and take the signed Wales Coast Path. This rises to cross the railway at a **level crossing**. Take the fenced Wales Coast Path ahead which shortly swings right to rise gently through woods.

A Ffestiniog Railway steam train crossing The Cob

3. Keep ahead at a **fork** and follow the steadily rising path through the trees. After swinging left, go through a large field gate and across the field towards a distant **farm** (Penrhyn Isaf). In the corner of the field turn left along a farm track.

In 1812 Penrhyn Isaf was the scene of a brutal murder committed by one of the workers on the construction of The Cob. A huge man known as Hwntw Mawr, broke into the house hoping to steal money and valuables but was disturbed by a maid, Mary Jones, whom he fatally stabbed in panic. He fled but was caught and publicly hanged in Dolgellau.

Continue past **farm buildings** and go ahead along a farm track. Immediately before a cattle grid, turn right at a junction of tracks. After a couple of gates you reach the edge of **Porthmeirion**, the famous Italianate village.

With no public access to Porthmeirion here, the right of way turns left keeping beside the fence to your right. When you reach a gate go ahead to reach a rough access road close to the house **Plas Canol**.

4. Passing the house, follow the access track and at a junction of farm tracks near **derelict farm buildings** take the signed

Fishing boats and yachts sheltering in Porthmadog Harbour

Wales Coast Path on the right. Enter a field keeping to the left edge and go through a gate in the far corner onto a woodland path. Walk ahead through the woods to reach a lane.

(To visit **Portmeirion village**, turn right and follow the driveway. Charges apply. Return to this point to continue the walk).

5. Cross over taking the signed bridleway opposite. At a T-junction turn left and walk along a rough lane with a grand view to the right across the Dwyryd estuary to the Rhinog hills.

In around 200 metres, opposite the gates to a house on the left, turn right through a footgate into a field. Walk down the field swinging left lower down to join an access track. Follow the track to the road in **Minffordd**. Turn left and follow the road through the village.

6. At the main road cross over taking the narrow lane opposite. Follow the lane downhill crossing the **railway line** and, at the bottom of the hill, turn left along a wider lane.

This lane follows what would have been the shoreline prior to the building of The Cob.

Follow this to meet the main road. Bear right along the pavement towards **Boston Lodge**.

Boston Lodge is so named because William Madocks was MP for Boston, Lincolnshire.

7. At the end of the lay-by, pass the **old Toll House** and join the footpath and cycleway. Retrace your steps across The Cob to back to Porthmadog to complete the walk.

As you enter Porthmadog keep ahead along the main street to reach **The Australia**. ♦

Portmeirion – Italianate village

Designed and built by eccentric architect, Sir Clough Williams-Ellis, between the 1920s and '70s, Portmeirion is a delightful, Italian Riviera-inspired fantasy village overlooking the broad Dwryd Estuary. The Rough Guide to Wales *calls it 'a gorgeous visual poem', and its brightly-painted arches, colonnades, piazzas and squares should delight even the most world-weary visitor. Portmeirion is open every day except Christmas Day.*

Useful Information

Wales Coast Path

Comprehensive information and maps for all sections of the Wales Coast Path can be found at www.walescoastpath.gov.uk. See also www.walescoastpath.co.uk

North Wales Tourist Information

Discover more about North Wales, Snowdonia National Park and the coast, from where to stay, what to do, events, and food and drink. See: **www.gonorthwales.co.uk**

Tourist Information Centres

The main TICs provide free information on everything from accommodation and transport to what's on and walking advice.

Chester	01244 405340	welcome@chestervic.co.uk
Rhyl	01745 355068	rhyl.tic@denbighshire.gov.uk
Llandudno	01492 577 577	llandudnotic@conwy.gov.uk
Conwy	01492 592248	conwytic@conwy.gov.uk
Bangor	01248 352786	bangor.tic@gwynedd.gov.uk

North Wales breweries and pubs

Oddly enough, it was the Sunday Closing Act of 1881 that helped shape Wales' unique 'Welshness', and it was only in 1996 that the last district, Dwyfor, abandoned 'Dry Sundays'. Before that, not a drop was drunk legally in Wales on the Sabbath.

Today, North Wales boasts both mainstream breweries like Wrexham Lager and a growing number of regional microbreweries, that include Conwy Brewery, Purple Moose - Porthmadog, Cwrw Llyn - Pwllheli, Nant Brewery - Llanrwst, and the Great Orme Brewery - Llandudno.

For details of the encouragingly high number of real ale pubs in North Wales, see the local CAMRA websites, or buy a copy of their excellent, annual **Good Beer Guide**.

Visitors can also sample many of the mouth-watering Welsh beers and ciders at festivals that include the Wrexham-based North Wales Beer & Cider Festival.

Weather

Online weather forecasts for the North Wales coast are available from the Met Office at **www.metoffice.gov.uk**